ONLY HERE
BECAUSE
HAVE NO
OTHER
OPTIONS

Want
to quit
and
never
return

FRIDAY
IS MY
SECOND
FAVORITE
F-WORD

All this time, and you haven't done sh*t

ANOTHER
SH*T
DAY
HERE

Can't stand the way you talk to me

INHALE
GOOD SH*T.
EXHALE
THE
BULLSH*T

Only
pretending
to be
interested
in
meeting

I gave
zero
f*cks
today

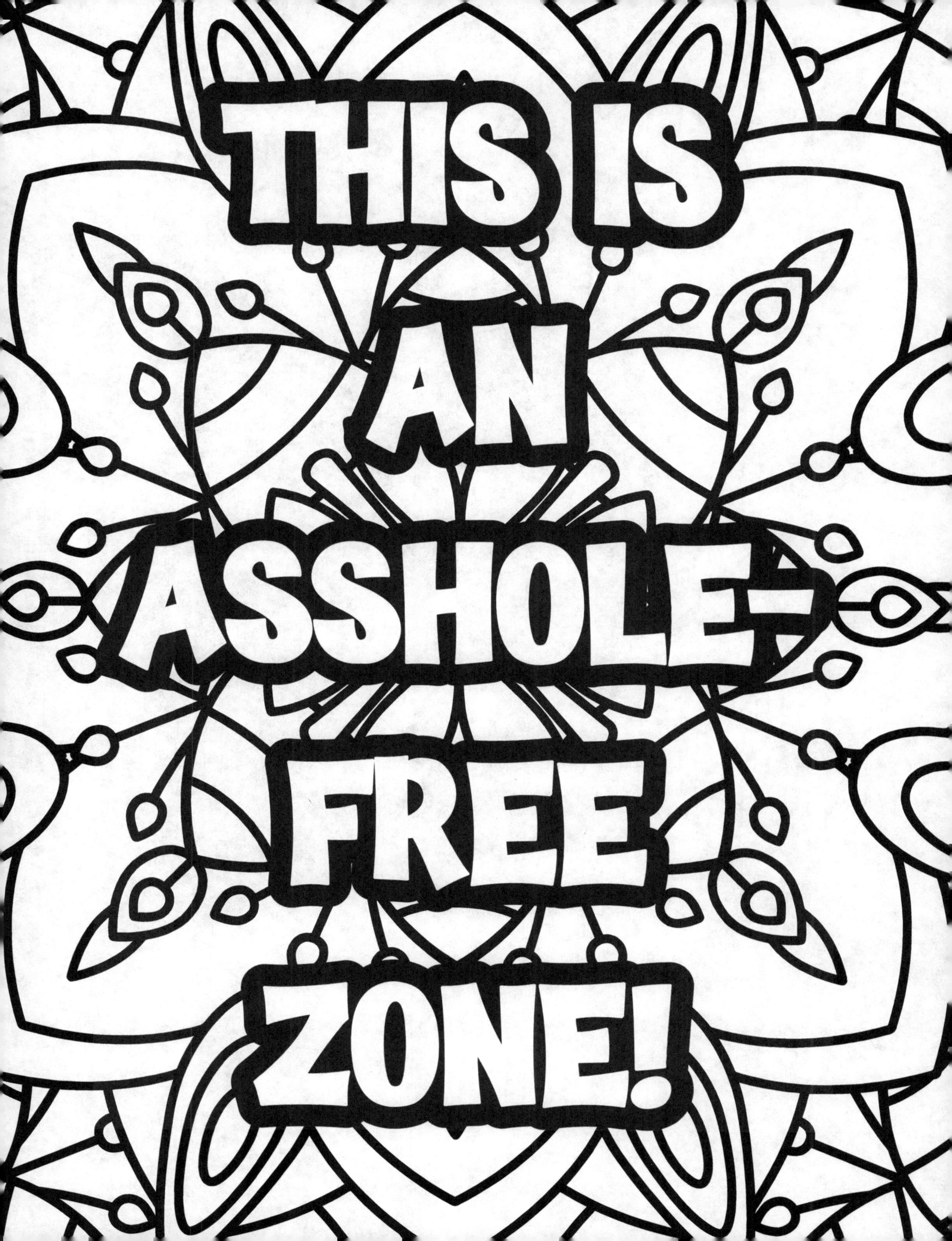
THIS IS
AN
ASSHOLE-
FREE
ZONE!

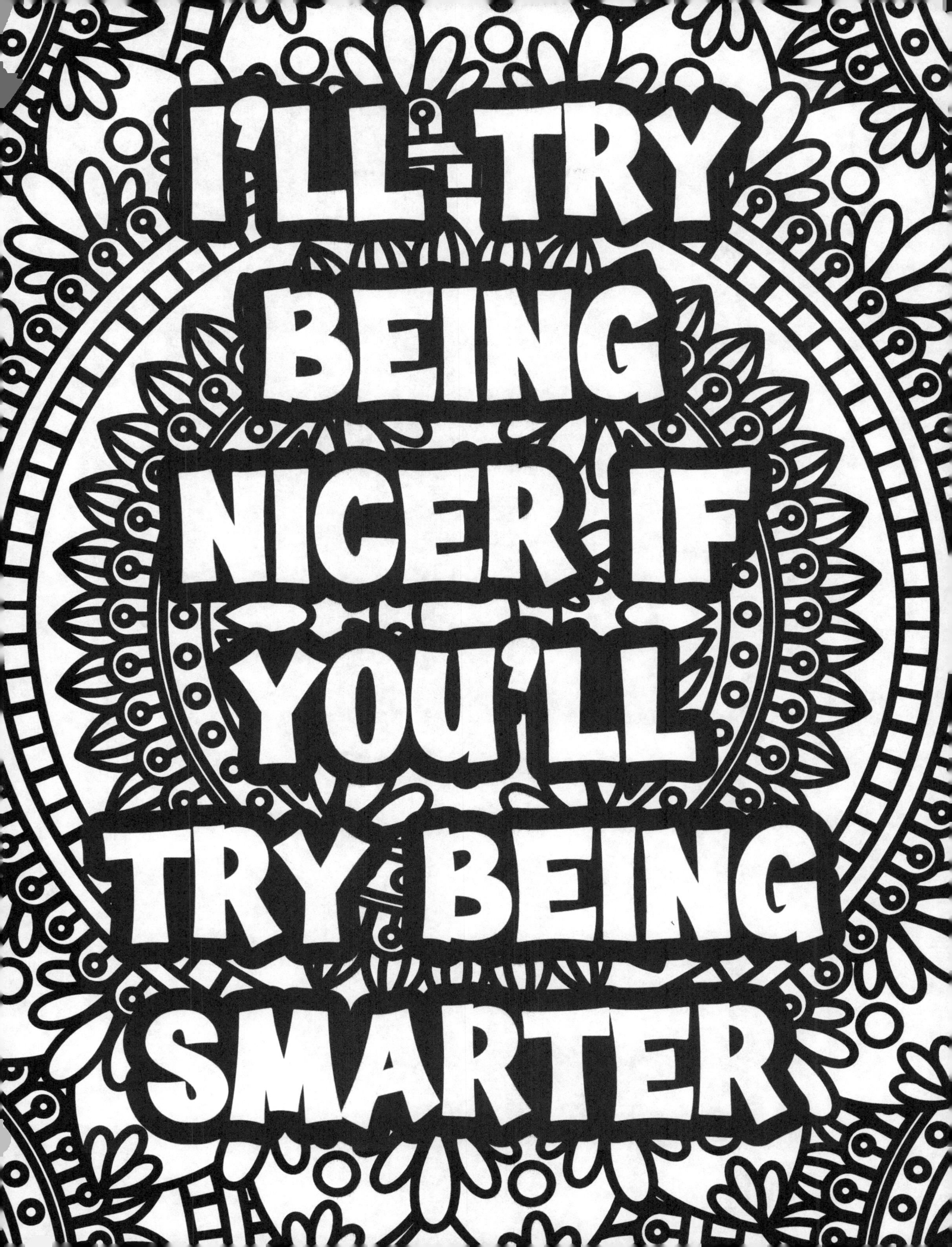
I'LL TRY
BEING
NICER IF
YOU'LL
TRY BEING
SMARTER

Secretly
looking
for
another
job

We
offer
free
courses
in crazy

CHEER
THE
F*CK UP

WHO THE
F*CK DIED
AND MADE
YOU
A BOSS?

Suck
my
D*ck

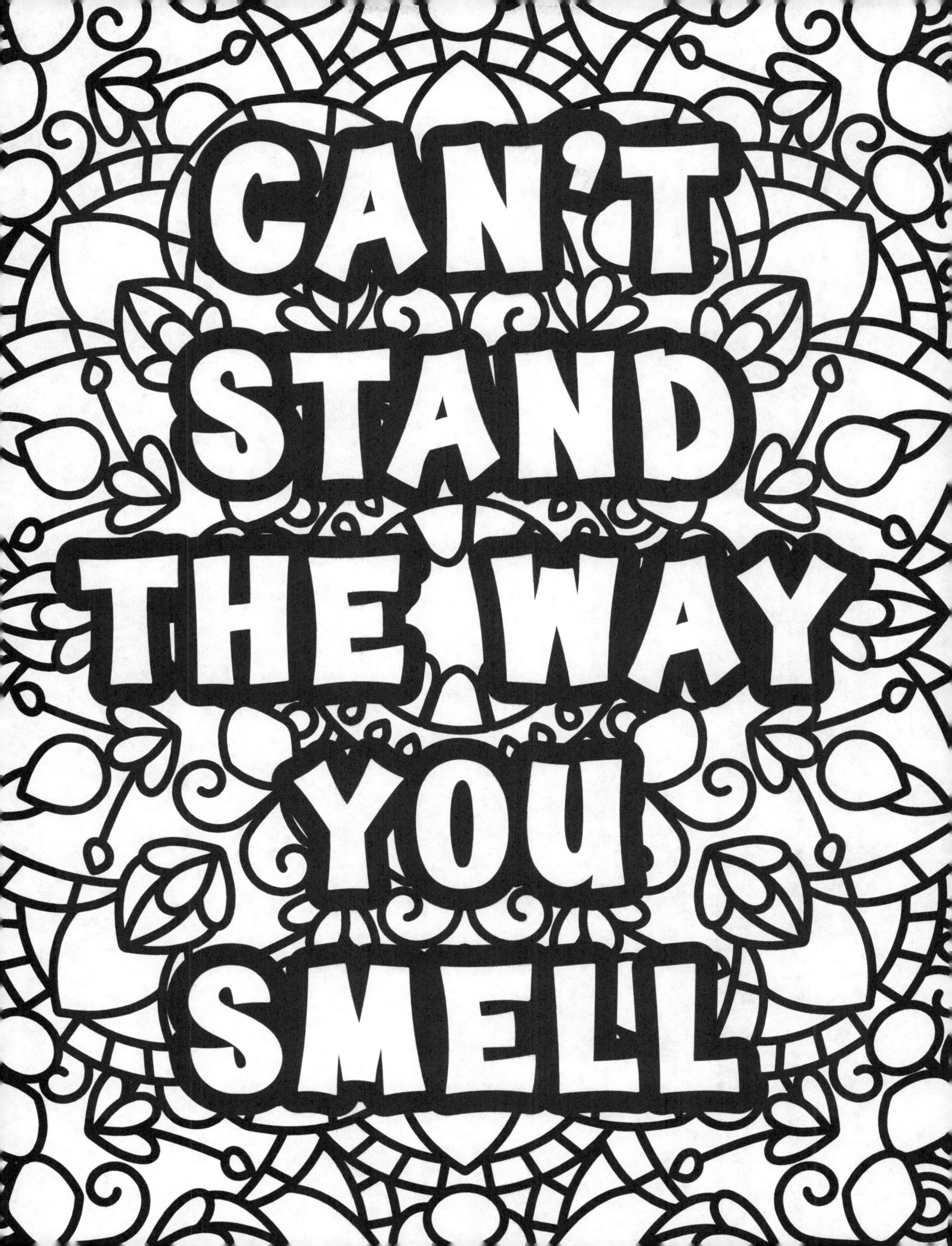
CAN'T
STAND
THE WAY
YOU
SMELL

Not a
f*cking
Monday
person

Who
the f*ck
moved
my
stapler?

CALM
THE
F*CK
DOWN

THINK
THE
COMPANY
WILL
FAIL

You inspire my inner serial killer

Another
sh*t
day
here

F*ck You

Sit
your
as*
down

SORRY
I CAN'T
WORK
TODAY

Why is the printer jammed?

DON'T
LIKE THE
WAY YOU
SPEAK
TO ME

CAN'T
STAND
WORKING
WITH
YOU

Worker?
I prefer
f*cking
rockstar

ZERO
F*CKS
GIVEN

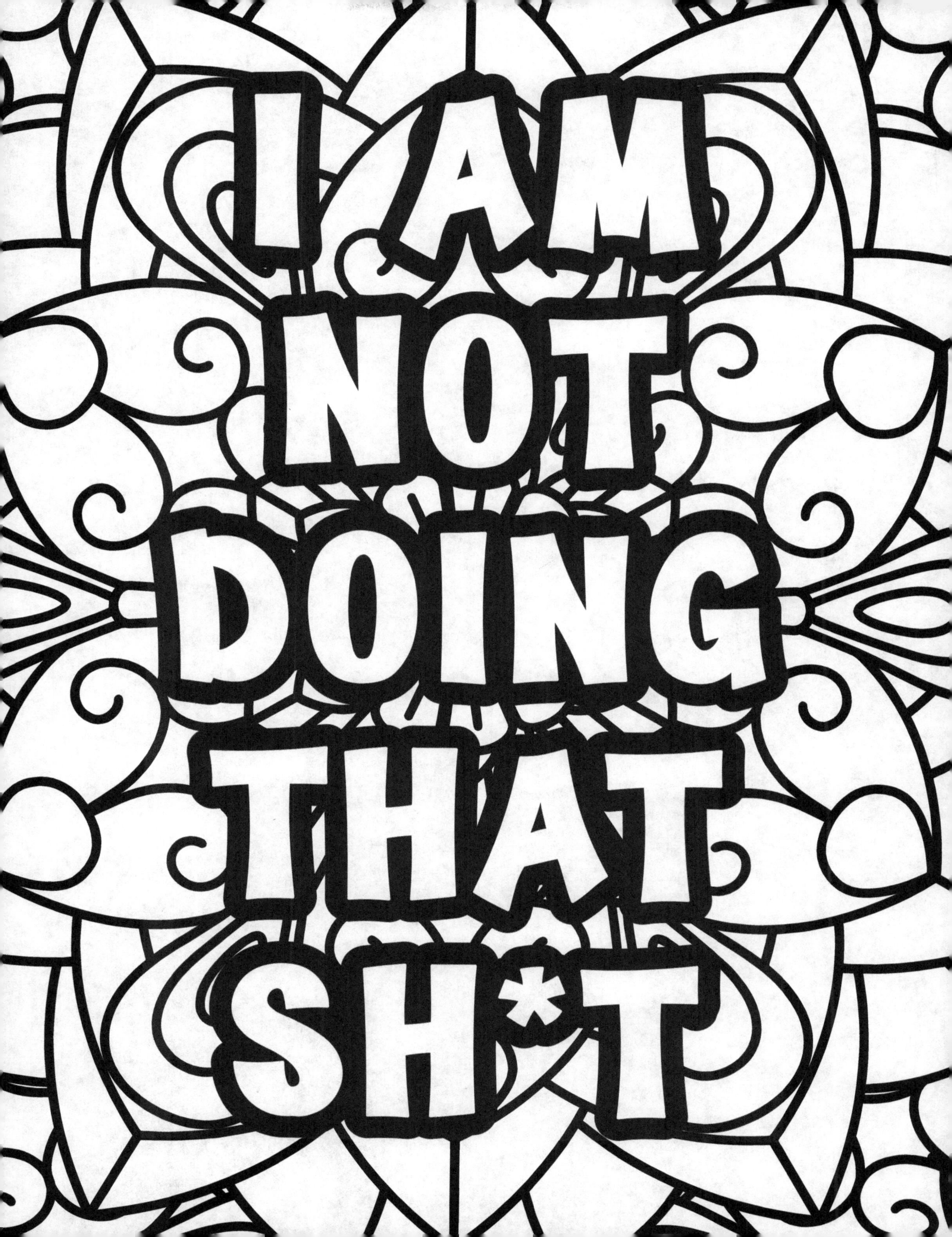
I AM
NOT
DOING
THAT
SH*T

I wish
I could
invoice
you for
wasting
my time

I need a mother-f*cking drink

STFU
Just
assume
I'm
always
right

I WISH
I COULD
IGNORE
YOU

WHAT
THE
F*CK
IS THAT
SH*T?

I'm
seriously
out of
f*cks
today

Sh*t!
Work
is
back

May
choke in
all the
sh*t
you talk

DON'T
BE
A
D*CK

Death
before
decaf

DON'T
THINK
YOU'RE
QUALIFIED

WANT
TO QUIT
AND
NEVER
RETURN

Is this
a
special
ed
class?!?

SECRETLY
LOOKING
FOR
ANOTHER
JOB

The
instant
worker
just
add
coffee

YOU
F*CKING
ROCK

WE OFFER FREE LESSONS IN CRAZY

I need
a huge
bottle
of
wine